Five Future Strategies You Need Right Now

Publisher's Note:
Memo to the CEO

Authored by leading experts and examining issues of special urgency, the books in the Memo to the CEO series are tailored for today's time-starved executives. Concise, focused, and solutions-oriented, each book explores a critical management challenge and offers authoritative counsel, provocative points of view, and practical insight.

Also available:

MEMO TO THE CEO

Five Future Strategies You Need Right Now

George Stalk

with John Butman

Harvard Business Press
Boston, Massachusetts

No part of this publication may be reproduced, stored in or introduced
into a retrieval system, or transmitted, in any form, or by any means
(electronic, mechanical, photocopying, recording, or otherwise), without
the prior permission of the publisher. Requests for permission should be
directed to permissions@hbsp.harvard.edu, or mailed to Permissions, Harvard
Business School Publishing, 60 Harvard Way, Boston, Massachusetts 02163.

Stalk, George, 1951–

    Five future strategies you need right now / George Stalk with John Butman.

       p.   cm. — (Memo to the CEO)

     ISBN 978-1-4221-2126-9

     1. Business logistics. 2. Strategic planning. 3. Competition. 4. Success in
business. I. Butman, John. II. Title.

    HD38.5.S73   2008

    658.4'012—dc22

                                       2007036565

The paper used in this publication meets the requirements of the American
National Standard for Permanence of Paper for Publications and Documents in
Libraries and Archives Z39.48-1992

Contents

Introduction
The Five Strategies

There are always important business issues forming like storm clouds on the horizon, but that are not yet so potent that they seem to demand your concerted attention. However, this is precisely the best time to focus on these issues and decide whether you should put more resources against them—right now. By doing so, you can gain an advantage over your competitors who haven't even glanced at the horizon yet or, if they have, are waiting to see what develops before they take any action. The danger is that, if you don't look ahead, those emerging wisps of vapor can rapidly turn into fast-moving thunderheads that hit before you've lifted a finger, especially if a competitor has taken action.

All too frequently I read in the business press about a new strategy miracle that underpins the rising fortunes of some company or executive, and I am struck by how out-of-date the story and the "news" really are. For example, I recently read a feature about the miracle of flexible manufacturing and how Chrysler, in an effort to lower costs, would be implementing a system that enabled the company to assemble more than one car platform on a single assembly line.

Miracle? Yes. New? No. Over twenty-five years ago, in 1981, Mazda opened its new Hofu plant outside of Hiroshima, Japan. The plant was designed to handle up to eight platforms. I know. I was there.

Time as a competitive weapon for manufacturers started gaining visibility in the late 1970s, but it's still being "discovered" as if it were invented yesterday.

Many innovations in strategy are like that—faint signals that gain strength until, years later, they appear in *BusinessWeek* or the *Wall Street Journal* and become commonplace. That's how it went with strategies based on experience, average costing, stalemate, and the new economics of information.

The hard part is figuring out which emerging strategic issues contain sufficient opportunity or significant-enough threat that they deserve attention now. That's where I hope to help.

My colleagues and I are in the habit of keeping "open files"—a repository of relevant information on some intriguing topic or issue—that we add to as new material becomes available. The topic usually comes to our attention as a "faint signal" but gradually becomes clearer as the file fills.

Sometimes a client will ask for help on one of our open issues. The file for supply chain gymnastics came into being when a client was approached by FastShip, Inc., which sought funding to develop jet-powered container ships. Our investigation into this very novel concept revealed the looming problems of demand and capacity imbalances in container shipping. That file quickly thickened.

I have three categories of open files:

1. **Faint signals:** Issues that will probably become strategies but have shown only a few, very slight, signs so far. A lot of development is needed.

2. **Watch list:** Potential strategies where the sources of competitive advantage are not entirely clear.

3. **Hallucinations:** Provocative issues that are so out there they may never materialize, or at least not within this lifetime.

The five strategies I'll discuss in this memo all began as faint signals, but the files on them are now sufficiently thick that the sources of advantage are not only abundantly clear, but undeniable:

- **Supply-chain gymnastics:** No, I'm not talking about your continuing efforts to lower production costs by outsourcing and off-shoring or even about the prospect of increased pressure from China-based competitors in worldwide markets. I'm referring to the increasingly thorny problem of managing your supply chain when it includes suppliers or partners in Asia, especially China, and how it affects your strategy. What's the problem? It's the yawning gap between demand for shipping and transit-related capabilities and the available supply. The very real possibility is that your goods or components will be caught in a "riptide" that can cost you time, money, market share, and opportunity. If you can swim against the tide while your competitors are treading water, significant competitive advantage awaits you.

- **Sidestepping economies of scale:** Although companies have long and correctly believed that achieving economies of scale is a sure path to greater volume and higher profits, companies in developing economies have explored new approaches to mass production that do not require access to capital or technology. The "disposable" factory, as I call it, is a labor-intensive, dedicated facility designed for temporary mass production with high throughput at low cost. As markets continue to become less predictable, and as product and even business life cycles become shorter, disposability can be an effective model even for companies that could take a more traditional route.

- **Dynamic pricing:** Most companies have been pretty diligent about improving their pricing through "good hygiene" practices like increasing list prices to match those of their competitors, enforcing special charges on custom orders, actively managing prices by customer, and others. These practices have yielded positive results, and must be continued. The next step, however, is to pursue dynamic pricing in which the company matches the price of its product or service with the immediate, second-by-second need of the customer who wishes to purchase and use it.

- **Embracing complexity:** "Simplification" is the mantra of many companies, especially after a business reaches a peak of model proliferation and feature complication that turned off consumers and put unnecessary burdens on producers. But now we're seeing four ways companies can attract those customers who are actually looking for a higher level of complexity and where such complexity represents an opportunity for share growth and increased profits. These are: heavy spenders, risk reducers, specifiers, and search engines.

- **Infinite bandwidth:** We're not there yet, but it won't be long before we live in a world where companies can effortlessly receive any amount of information they want, in any form they need, at any time and place, and at zero cost. When that world materializes (or perhaps I should say dematerializes), some companies will be ready to take advantage of their newfound power and capability, others will not. There are three important areas in which infinite bandwidth can create competitive advantage: increasing operational efficiencies, creating new business models, and establishing whole new businesses.

These issues may still seem to be faint signals to you. But like so many emerging issues of the past fifty years—including the strategies I've already mentioned—these are likely to appear on the front pages of the business press before you know it.

Introduction

In *Five Future Strategies You Need Right Now*, I offer a high-level introduction to each of these emerging issues, along with suggestions for how to turn them into competitive advantage.

Supply Chain Gymnastics

In the past several years, I've watched as companies have become highly skilled at performing what I call *supply chain gymnastics*—outsourcing, subcontracting, partnering, offshoring, bestshoring, and all the rest, primarily in China. Today, many companies source 50 percent or more of their goods from Asia and, as a result, have lowered their costs, increased profits, and built share.

However, there is a real emergency in the making that threatens to put at risk all the benefits companies have realized (and still are realizing) from their supply-chain efforts. I'm speaking of the shipping- and freight-related infrastructure issues on the West Coast of the United States and in Western Europe.

The problem, in short, is that the huge surge of goods arriving on our shores from China and elsewhere in Asia could easily overwhelm the infrastructure that receives and distributes them. Just one prediction puts the problem in perspective: the West Coast ports of the United States will reach their combined container unloading and loading capacity as early as 2010.

This phenomenon, which I call the *China riptide*, will suck away the savings that companies think they are achieving through China sourcing by dramatically adding new costs that are difficult to anticipate and tricky to manage. And while I say China, I could just as well be talking about Vietnam, Thailand, or Korea. China imports just happen to be at the center of the storm at the moment.

You might think that this is a rather simple and limited issue of shipping and distribution, but the problem is significant enough to have serious implications for the way you do business and the strategies you pursue. As we'll see, supply chain and strategy are intricately linked.

Many companies I work with are well aware of parts of the problem and have been doing what they can to prepare for even more stress on the system—increasing inventories, accepting longer lead times, and redoubling efforts to forecast more accurately. Others have shifted more of their goods transfer from surface to air freight, raising prices when they can to absorb the increased costs. I regret to say that,

as useful as these efforts are, they are not enough—
they will not forestall the problem and can, in some
cases, aggravate the situation.

The Emergency

Companies that source manufactured goods from
China (and our data shows that the majority of the
Fortune 1000 fit that description) do so primarily because of the attractive production costs. For the most
part, the efforts have paid off, and companies have
seen their costs go down (with help from steadily de-
clining on-ocean logistics costs) and margins rise.
Now, however, cost advantages are harder to come
by. Companies have reached a point at which there is
little cost remaining to be squeezed out of the on-
ocean shipping process. In fact, on-ocean costs typically now account for only about 1 percent of retail
shelf price.

Businesses might have continued to surf this wave,
squeezing out a few more pennies of the on-ocean
costs as larger ships were brought into the fleet and
off-loading processes were made even more efficient,
if the wave had not continued to grow. The first serious indication of trouble was an eight-day lockout of
dockworkers in 2002, which shut down the West
Coast ports. Then in the fall of 2004, the operations

at the ports of Los Angeles/Long Beach, where over 40 percent of the containers from Asia enter the United States, nearly ground to a halt as all the systems involved—harbors, cranes, trucks, and trains—were unable to keep up with the surge of arriving containers. Almost one hundred ships lay at anchor waiting for berths, and then languished many more days at dockside before they could be unloaded. I estimate that those delays in off-loading cost some companies as much as 5 cents per share.

People focused on the obvious message of the strike—how dependent on imported goods from China the U.S. economy has become—but paid less attention to the underlying problem: that the ocean (and rail) freight infrastructure on the West Coast of the United States had come under severe strain. What we should have learned from the strike is just how dependent we are on a small number of ports, how easily the operations of those ports can be disrupted, and how huge an impact such a disruption can have on operations.

Since the strike, the infrastructure problems have become increasingly evident in the day-to-day operations of most companies. More and more shipments arrive behind schedule at their distribution centers. Logistics and marketing people ask for increased levels of inventories to protect the company against stock-outs, but stock-outs continue nonetheless. Weeks have been added to the replenishment cycle. And all too often companies find that they have to mark down excess inventories in order to move them. Companies can usually track these costs. Rarely can they or do they track the lost profits of not having the goods they could have sold had the logistic systems been responsive.

And it's only going to get worse.

The amount of goods arriving in containers from Asia, especially China, has accelerated rapidly in the last few years and is now growing so fast—at 9 to 12 percent per year—that even the world's fleet of monster container ships cannot keep up with the increase. Indeed, the incremental inbound flow of containers to the United States is equivalent to about one Port of Vancouver a year (1.5 million containers).

The result, as I said at the outset, is that the West Coast ports will be overwhelmed and could max out their combined container-handling capacity by 2010. Meanwhile, China is increasing its ability to fill ships with goods. Over the next several years, some one hundred new container-loading berths will be built in China, each with a lift capacity of about 250,000 containers per year.

Operators of North American ports say they understand the challenge and vow they will increase their port capacity. There are only two ways to do so, however, and both have their problems. The first is to enlarge the dockside footprint, but any significant expansion is likely to be opposed by the communities in which the ports operate, and their protests could very well cause significant delays in port expansions or prevent them altogether. (I may be the only person on earth who sees ports as things of beauty!) The other way to increase capacity would be to significantly improve productivity, but to do that would require a breakthrough in labor-management relations that is unlikely in an environment that has a long history of discord.

Even increasing port capacity through either one of these methods would only push off the day of reckoning for three to five years, given the growth rate of the number of containers inbound from Asia. If ports could do both—expand their footprints *and* achieve productivity improvements—the unhappy day might be postponed for eight to nine years at most.

Another way to alleviate the pressure would be to develop other ports that are currently underutilized or to build entirely new ones. But even in the best-case scenarios, significant new capacity at such ports could not come online for many years, and even then their capacity would be inadequate to meet the emerging need.

So, for at least the next decade, we're going to be swimming against the tide.

The Economics

How does this situation affect the economics of the China supply chain and the strategies for exploiting it?

First, it's important to understand that every supply chain involves two types of profits—accounting and economic—and three types of costs—direct, indirect, and hidden. As a supply chain gets longer and more complex and involves more time, direct, indirect, and hidden costs proliferate and their magnitude increases, which causes accounting profits and economic profits to diverge.

Typically, the direct and indirect costs associated with a supply chain can equal from 4 to 8 percent of the retail shelf cost of any item. Direct costs include shipping; nesting and de-nesting of containers at both ends of the ocean pipeline; as well as inventory storage, handling, and procurement. Indirect costs include insurance and overall financing. Although these costs vary, and are increased or decreased by the length and complexity of the chain, they are relatively easy to identify.

It's the hidden costs of a long supply chain that are the real killers. The most important one is the gross margin a company loses when it doesn't have a product that is selling in stock. (Gross margin can range from 40 to 60 percent of the retail shelf price.) This can happen when the product is in the hold of a ship, stuck in a container, sitting on a rail spur somewhere, or wasn't actually ordered at all to meet the changing demands of the market. This drives down economic profits while accounting profits may still look good.

Not having product to sell is the most damaging hidden cost, but having too much inventory of a product that is *not* selling comes a close second. The write-down costs of excess inventory average out to 10 to 20 percent of retail shelf price.

A company that can avoid the lost margins of stock-outs and overstocks earns more money than the one that can't. This is money that can be used to gain strategic advantage through other investments in the business.

At many companies, however, managers believe that these problems come about as the result of forecasting errors, rather than fluctuations in the supply chain. When inventory levels are not optimal, management's response is to try to forecast even farther into the future—predicting demand and seeking to freeze orders as far in advance as possible. But supply-chain fluctuations only increase when the time span gets longer, so a longer-term forecast will likely be less accurate and more seriously affected by the dynamics of the system.

Another hidden cost—which is not caused by supply-chain fluctuations but is made worse by them—is the expense of finding and removing defective inventory from the supply chain. It takes time to identify the cause of a quality problem, determine how to correct it, and then adjust production to fix it. During the time it takes to conduct your detective work, the problem goods continue to be fed into the chain. Not only will there be costs associated with finding and fixing the defective inventory, there will be additional costs required to produce new goods to meet back orders and current demand and to physically replace the subpar goods with new product throughout the chain.

Finally, supply-chain fluctuations can affect your company—even if your company is able to maintain the optimal inventory levels—if you operate in a category of goods in which other companies work with long supply chains. Chances are that one or more of them will not be so expert at managing the supply chain and will have too little or too much inventory in the pipeline. If there is too little inventory in the category, you may be pressured to produce more supply quickly. If there is too much inventory category-wide, your company may find itself in a retail pricing battle. So, even if you're incredibly accurate in your forecasting and get the inventory right, the fluctuations in the supply chain can still cause problems.

There's nowhere to hide.

The Strategic Implications

Now that Asia sourcing is a standard business practice, the issue is how well you manage the supply chain—particularly the hidden costs and lost profits—rather than which countries you source from. I have run complex simulations comparing China-based supply chains with domestic supply chains and found that most companies, in most categories, can gain a cost advantage over their competitors with either one. (Again, while I reference China, this finding applies to any supply chain that includes distant components.)

The key is information management; and the longer and more sophisticated the chain, the more important the integration of information becomes.

I define three levels of supply-chain management:

- **The *nonintegrated* supply chain:** In this type of chain, each upstream step gets its information on demand from its customer on the next step of the chain. Fluctuations are difficult to see, manage, and change. Management usually learns about overstocks, understocks, or sub-par products from the final link in the chain— usually the retail outlet. This typically means that the full span of time is required to correct a problem.

- The *semi-integrated* supply chain: In this chain, each step gets its information on customer demand from its customer two steps down— usually from one or more distribution centers on either side of the ocean. Fluctuations are more evident and can be better managed. Still, to correct a problem requires more time than it should or could.

- The *integrated* supply chain: In a chain with the highest level of sophistication, each step in the chain has a full view of final customer demand. Fluctuations are almost immediately evident and companies can more easily and quickly respond to them.

The advantage gained by moving from one level to another turns supply-chain gymnastics into a group sport. For example, let's suppose that Company A moves from a domestic sourcing strategy to a

China-based, nonintegrated supply chain. Management soon discovers the difficulties of managing the nonintegrated chain and moves to a semi-integrated state. Its operating margin improves.

With its costs reduced, Company A decides to cut the retail unit price in order to gain share from its archrival, Company B, which operates a domestic supply chain. Company B chooses to defend its share by matching Company A's price cut, even though the reduction will turn its operating margin into a per unit loss.

After letting Company B bleed for a while, Company A decides it has enough margin that it can cut its per unit price again. The margin will decline, yes, but the company will still make a profit on each unit, thanks to its combination of low unit product cost and semi-integrated information flow.

The games could continue indefinitely. Company B would gain back its advantage if it could fully integrate its information flow and if it could also cut end-to-end cycle times by half (which, admittedly, is a big *if* for many companies). With that enhanced responsiveness, Company B's domestic chain would be more in stock and less in overstock, and its operating margin would increase. Its combination of integrated information and reduced cycle time would give it the advantage over Company A, lumbering along with a semi-integrated supply chain and longer cycle times. Company B would make a profit on each unit.

Company A could, of course, strike back by fully integrating its China-based supply chain and cutting its cycle time in half, and would gain back the advantage thanks to its lower unit cost.

Maybe. The China riptide adds a new current to the dynamics of the game. Generally, cycle times of the China-based supply chains are going up, not down. If they increased from eleven weeks to eighteen weeks, as they have for some retailers and manufacturers of durable goods, the China-based chains would suffer a decline in operating margin, experiencing a growing number of stock-outs or running more overstocks, while the domestic chains with higher levels of sophistication would still be realizing a profit.

That's not all. The cycle times of surface shipments (from China to Chicago, for example) are not only lengthening, but the fluctuations are also increasing. About 50 percent of the containers at one shipping company are off-loaded within one week of their scheduled dates, and these deliveries are considered (by the shipping companies, at least) to be on time. The other 50 percent are even less predictable!

If the stated delivery time of eighteen weeks can randomly vary six weeks either way, the company with a semi-integrated China-based supply chain will lose operating margin. The implication is that it is possible for a domestic supply chain with integrated information flows and fast cycle times to outperform a China-based chain, despite China's lower unit product cost.

It's not just about where you source anymore. It's how well you do it.

Courses of Action

What actions should you take to become as efficient as possible?

First, assess your operations and processes. For the parts of your business that aren't currently sourcing from China or elsewhere in Asia, I recommend the following steps:

- Reduce minimum-production-order quantities and reduce cycle times as quickly and as much as possible.

- Refrain from sourcing or manufacturing in China until you fully understand the dynamics of the supply chains.

- Create an integrated or a semi-integrated information flow within the company's existing supply chain.

- Conduct in-depth examinations of buying practices and management of supplier relationships at all levels of the supply chain in order to identify areas where hidden costs could arise and to prevent their occurrence.

- Separate the flows of orders through the supply chain on the basis of order predictability and demand volatility so that components with the highest gross margins and the most volatile demand get the fastest handling.

In short, be operationally more effective than your competitors in your sourcing and supply-chain management. Don't just do as well as they do—do much better. Be competitively advantaged.

For those parts of your business that currently do source from or manufacture in China, you should explore alternatives that will minimize adverse supply-chain effects, including options that might appear costly at first but may result in overall lower costs. For example:

- Use air freight for products with the highest margins and volatility. Air freight can be four to six times more expensive than surface freight, but the costs are still lower than the costs of stock-outs and overstocks. If you are aggressive, you may be able to lock up capacity at the best rates, forcing your competitors into a higher-cost, spot market.

- Insist on point-to-point ocean shipping. To reduce costs, shipping companies are building larger and larger container carriers, which must be scheduled to call on multiple ports. Shipping products on a vessel that has your destination as its last port of call can add weeks—and great variability—to transit times. Look for schedules that result in your goods being the last loaded and first unloaded. Let your competitors get the best rates on the "slow boats from China."

- Develop better relationships with transportation providers. This could mean identifying opportunities to speed the movement of goods, often by paying shippers and handlers for preferential treatment. In *hot hatching*, for example, you offer a premium to a shipper that will load your goods onto its vessel last and unload them first. Another option is to work with the few shipping companies able to off-load containers directly onto rail cars that head east on an express basis—cutting days and sometimes weeks out of the supply chain. Again, do this before your competitors do it.

All these initiatives require investment in one of two forms: in premiums or in capabilities. Premiums are the extra payments required to get substantially enhanced performance and preferred treatment from suppliers like ground, sea, and air shippers and port services. Companies can get results by forcing suppliers to compete on service in return for premiums.

Investments in capabilities, which tend to be a good deal harder to discern and carry out, include:

- Accelerating the flow and interpretation of information

- Developing designs that enable final assembly to take place close to the point of final demand, thereby minimizing the time and cost effects of long supply chains

- Learning to source, manufacture, launch, and withdraw products more effectively

- Exploiting new concepts for fast freight with your brokers, liner companies, rail carriers and truckers

Identifying these strategic investment opportunities requires exhaustive investigation and analysis of costs, revenues, and lost margins in today's end to end supply chains. You need to ask, what if? And you need to explore each answer thoroughly before deciding that no additional investment in premiums and capabilities is likely to produce further improvement. You need to be especially alert to the subtle but important system effects of investing at one part of the chain to affect performance at another.

Information is power, and you need to invest in it. Here are six information-related steps you can take to improve your supply chain:

- Estimate the size of the prize and make sure you seriously consider all viable options (including Mexico and Central Eastern Europe (CEE) for Western Europe). How will the ideas discussed in this memo work in these different environments? What are their special situations: High volatility? Fast fashion cycles? Customization? Distributed manufacturing?

- "Walk the line." Figure out what is actually happening and why, step by step, from your customer all the way through your supply chain.

- Focus on dramatically improving the responsiveness and reliability of key participants in the supply chain. Sometimes simple procedural changes can have huge implications.

- Identify and vet the changes necessary within the organization and across the supply chain to realize opportunities. Companies are seldom organized to make the cross-functional changes required to materially impact a supply chain's performance. One company's purchasing group sourced the parts for a particular design from suppliers in three different countries solely on the basis of unit production costs (UPCs) and without regard for the system impact of the decision. The result was frequent assembly shortages and emergency air-freight charges.

- Get information to the top of your company. Push efforts onto the A list of priorities of the company's leadership—or else abandon the effort altogether. Dramatically improved supply-chain performance, like any activity that affects strategy, can't happen without a mandate from leadership. Otherwise, the near-term and narrowly focused performance parameters of the organization will bring all sustained effort to a halt.

- Build improvement efforts into your operating plans and budgets throughout your company. Some organizations simply build in stretch performance goals and let their business units rush to find solutions. This method is scary to watch, but it can be very effective.

In general—and of utmost importance—your strategy must match your approach to the supply chain. A company that decides not to source goods in China while its competitor does can sometimes override its rival's direct cost advantage by increasing that rival's logistical disadvantage. For example, what if the company with the domestic supply chain is able to increase the degree of customization its customers want or raise the fashion quotient—more variety or more frequent selling seasons—in some category of its business? In that case, the demand volatility for certain products will be increased and the China-anchored competitor, with its long lead times, could find its logistical problems aggravated.

Companies with time-advantaged supply chains might also consider consignment pricing, requiring their wholesale customers to pay only when they sell the company's products. To match this appealing offer to customers, competitors with a much longer supply chain will have to incur much higher costs for carrying greater inventory.

A Final Thought

The current problems of sourcing in China act, in effect, as a giant nontariff trade barrier. In fact, the best strategy for U.S. protectionists may lie not in quotas or tariffs but in the active backing of environmentalists' efforts to hinder port expansion.

As I've said, the situation is likely to get worse before it gets better. Politicians throughout the United States and Canada will dither and debate until world events overtake them and their options for alleviating the port bottlenecks have vanished.

Companies will do what they can—and in this memo, I've suggested a number of approaches—but a single corporation can do little to solve the broader problem. An increasingly frustrated China, which has the most to lose from this de facto trade barrier, may undertake a major initiative, such as developing a new port on the west coast of Mexico. Any such effort would take years to have an effect, but the possibility is real.

If your company is operating and selling from Europe and North America, it will not be easy to get your situation right. Winning will require creativity

and insight into customer behavior as well as seg
mented options, detailed cost analysis, spending money
on one part of the supply chain to improve performance in other parts (various members of your
functional organization will undoubtedly scream
about this!), and practicing the kind of management
that many executive teams will view as an out-of-
body experience. Yet the problem is severe enough
that *someone* out there is undoubtedly trying to do
something about it.

I encourage you to be that someone.

Sidestepping
Economies of Scale

Let's suppose that your business is doing well. Your company is growing and expects to see additional growth as you launch more and more products and service. Many of your new offerings carry healthy margins.

Still, is something wrong with this picture?

Your ability to accurately forecast the demand for your new products and services is, in a word, terrible. Your people tell you, "We overestimate demand as often we underestimate it, especially in the early years of a product's life. Some of our offerings carry on for a remarkably long period, giving us plenty of time to amortize our investment. Others blossom quickly but wither just as fast. Then we're left with equipment and people far in excess of what we need and that can be difficult to repurpose."

Fortunately your competitors are no better at forecasting or deployment than you are, so if you can find a safe way to create greater flexibility, you have a chance to create competitive advantage. Unfortunately, you may be frustrated in finding that way because of your belief in the power of economies of scale. The belief that bigger is better—that scale automatically means low costs—is widespread among strategists. But as today's markets become increasingly volatile and therefore difficult to forecast, many business leaders are reexamining their assumptions about the benefits of scale.

There is another route to lowering overall costs and avoiding the missteps that come from faulty forecasting: the disposable factory. When choosing among craft, batch, and mass modes of manufacturing, a company must weigh the value of scale against the potential for market shortfalls. How sure can we be that a particular volume of product X will find a market within time period Y? As the expected rate of profitable production rises, the answer shifts from small-scale, one-at-a-time craft production to batch production and ultimately to mass production.

Disposable factories provide a low-risk means of jumping in and out of fast-moving markets. They offer investment flexibility through production inflexibility.

In this memo, I'll show how companies in a range of sectors (manufacturing and also services) are benefiting from the disposable factory mind-set. And I'll provide suggestions for maximizing the strategic value beyond manufacturing of this approach.

Sometimes, as we'll see, it pays to think small.

The Emergency

The belief in the power of economies of scale can be especially frustrating in markets that are highly volatile and difficult to forecast—and there is plenty of evidence to show that many markets fit that description. Demand forecasts for a new pharmaceutical can easily be off by as much as −75 percent to +300 percent in the first couple of years after introduction. Product life cycles are shortening dramatically: the average life of a new car platform has declined from nearly eight years almost twenty years ago to about four years today. The life of a cell phone has declined from about twenty-two months just six years ago to sixteen months today. And the "fashion" life of a personal computer has gone from four years to one.

Of course, the worst form of volatility occurs when a new product or service bombs. An oft-quoted finding states that of the thirty thousand new consumer products launched each year, over 90 percent of them eventually fail. Research conducted by my colleagues shows that for products with launch budgets of more than $25 million, a mere 20 percent are regarded as successes.

As market volatility has increased, executives have begun doing more than just reassessing the supposed benefits of scale. Some have also begun steering clear of it entirely. New technology and management methods have helped to drive this phenomenon. For example, information technology has substantially reduced the size of the lowest-cost unit of data processing, enabling desktop workstations to handle the same volume of work formerly done by mainframes. And just-in-time manufacturing (first introduced in Japan) is helping more organizations operate factories that are smaller than those of their competitors. These smaller factories put out more complex product offerings at higher levels of quality and productivity than larger facilities. For instance, the world-scale automotive assembly facility has gone from producing two hundred thousand units a year to fewer than fifty thousand, and programmable machining centers and robotics used in these plants have squeezed more labor out of the manufacturing process and further reduced the lowest-cost unit of scale.

Meanwhile, another phenomenon that my colleagues and I call *deconstruction* has further opened executives' eyes to alternatives to scale. Historically, companies were vertically integrated so they could manage the information required to do business. The bigger the vertically integrated business was in comparison to its competitors, the lower its costs tended to be. But with advances in information technology and the creation of intermediate markets between links in the value chains the value of size came into question. Vertically integrated companies in industries as diverse as newspapers, computers, telecommunications, pharmaceuticals, and electric utilities deconstructed themselves.

Peering Inside the Disposable Factory

Scale can be a double-edged sword, and the disposable factory can help you avoid getting cut by it.

The disposable factory is a manufacturing operation that is built as inexpensively as possible with the primary purpose of getting a new product into the market. It can have a higher cost of manufacture than if you had allowed engineers and suppliers to build the best facility to meet hypothetical demand. But in the grand scheme of things, the cost penalty is usually small, and, in return, you get a lot of flexibility.

Because it is disposable, it is easy to get rid of the operation if the market demand isn't what you expected. If the market is there, you can still throw out the factory and replace it with another one, built to be as low-cost and as flexible as the market tells you it needs to be. Because the disposable factory is so simple to create, you can save valuable time getting to market and reduce the capital risk of overestimating the demand. With this combination of increased revenues and reduced costs, you're sure to see a measurable improvement in your bottom line—and gain a considerable advantage over your competitors.

The disposable factory is not a new idea. It has long been the favored approach in project-oriented industries where there is great uncertainty and where large numbers of a product need to be manufactured quickly. You can see examples of disposable factories in many high-risk endeavors—they're the field messes on movie sets and battlefields, temporary concrete-making facilities set up next to large engineering works, and cocaine laboratories in the jungle. But sophisticated businesspeople have turned up their noses at this kind of "wildcatting" because they have been so long in the thrall of the economies-of-scale doctrine.

Now, smart companies are considering disposable manufacturing in a wide variety of process-based industries— like chemicals and pharmaceuticals—as well.

One large pharmaceutical company had spent years building a significant position in global markets for a complex pharmaceutical ingredient, but the position had been challenged by lower-cost competitors based in China. Although the company had superior production technology and much more experience than its Chinese rivals, it was losing share to them.

The pharma company's facilities were highly automated and engineered for low costs from large-scale, flexible production. The equipment cost hundreds of millions of dollars and had a thirty-year life cycle. Such a plant constitutes a substantial bet on the longevity of a product category and a company's position in that category.

But companies in the rapidly developing economies—China, India, Russia, Brazil, and others—have not had the luxuries of capital and technology that make such large-scale production possible. So, in order to compete, they have adapted to market challenges by building small, labor-intensive, short-lived plants designed for temporary, low-cost mass production. They operate with a fixed capacity geared to one product (and a specific quantity of that product) rather than adjusting capacity to produce a range of batch sizes or product types. Put another way, they are built to satisfy actual, not forecasted, demand.

A Chinese disposable facility can be built for as little as 20 to 30 percent of the cost of a typical plant in the United States or Europe. The components are simple and locally sourced. Instead of computer-controlled process-monitoring equipment, the Chinese facilities rely on visual inspection by workers, which is backed up by more visual inspection of the visual inspectors.

Such plants can be constructed with remarkable speed. With basic engineering and construction techniques, a disposable factory can be erected in as little as six months—a huge improvement over the twenty-four to thirty-six months that the approval and construction process would take in the United States or Europe.

When we've asked the Chinese players how they manage to fill orders with inexpensive equipment in cheaply built, inflexible plants, they answer, "If the equipment fails, no big deal. We can swap it out, tear it down, or build another plant for the next product."

The Chinese think of plants like ball-point pens. When it breaks or runs out of ink, toss it.

From Disposal Factory to Disposable Strategy

The disposable factory model is valuable in many aspects of business—not just process- or project-oriented manufacturing. In fast-changing environments, any number of a business's elements may prove disposable, including organizational structures, management teams, distribution channels, and even strategies. In a recent survey quoted in *Harvard Business Review*, of

"259 senior executives [interviewed] around the world
. . . more than 80 percent of them indicated that the
productive lives of their strategies were getting shorter.
Seventy-two percent believed that their leading competitor would be a different company in five years."[1]

More and more frequently, companies are finding
that their "great strategies" are at risk of being made
obsolete before they get a chance to prove out. So
businesses must find ways to think of their strategies
as disposable as well.

Orbitz, the online travel agent, is an example of a
company that built a kind of disposable factory, even
though it didn't manufacture a tangible product. In
late 1999, during a period of slow growth for the air-
line industry, five major U.S. airlines—Delta, United,
American, Northwest, and Continental—joined forces
to create an online travel site. The strategy was for
the site to have such low distribution costs that airlines would find it financially attractive to show all of
their publicly available inventory, unlike Travelocity
and other online travel services that showed only a
partial inventory of flights. That would ensure that
Orbitz could offer the best deals that Delta, United,
American, Northwest, and Continental offered anywhere, including on their own Web sites or through
third-party travel distributors. In addition, Orbitz in-

tended to use a sophisticated search technology that would convince customers that the fares they found on the site were the lowest available, because so much current and reliable information was displayed.

The strategies sounded good, but there was no guarantee they would be successful. The company had to grow extremely fast if it were to join Travelocity and Expedia in the leadership ranks, satisfy the profit goals of some of its owners, and ensure a future for itself.

But there was no company that the airlines could acquire that had the right characteristics and could be purchased at an acceptable price. The partners doubted that incubating the new service inside one of the sponsoring organizations would work because, although the airlines were partners in this venture, they were also competitors. Plus, based on their experiences in building new, low-cost airlines from within the ranks of a legacy organization, they knew how difficult it could be to cut the fledgling company loose from the parent when the time came. They also realized that the traditional start-up approach— building the organization one employee at a time— would take far too long.

Orbitz had to find a different way into the market, and it did. The company assembled a temporary management team comprising a few internal professionals plus more than sixty participants from a number of external partners and suppliers—including consulting, law, accounting, engineering, and human resource firms. They were, in essence, equivalent to the locally sourced, single-task manufacturing components of a disposable factory. They were not necessarily the lowest-cost people available, in terms of compensation, but their commitment and capabilities were such that they could be rapidly and almost effortlessly redeployed.

This worked. In less than two years, Orbitz was serving customers and proving itself as a competitor. So, just like a Chinese manufacturer that replaces its subscale, inflexible, and high-cost factories as markets prove out, Orbitz did the same with its temporary management team—eventually all the temporary, highly capable but high-cost resources were swapped out with permanent, more finely matched resources.

The disposable strategy paid big dividends for its owners. The site launched in June 2001 and, according to Nielsen/Net Ratings, it was the biggest e-commerce launch since 1999, with 2.07 million unique at-home visitors to the site during the month of June. In 2003, an Orbitz IPO valued the company at nearly $1 billion and, in 2004, the airlines agreed to sell Orbitz to

Cendant for $1.25 billion, which put more than $1 billion into their pockets.

Courses of Action

Given the benefits of disposable factories (actual and metaphorical), how can you get the most strategic advantage from this approach? Start by deciding whether the model is right for you.

It's the appropriate choice under the following circumstances:

- Speed, risk, and the need for particular assets make alternative production models uneconomical.

- You face extreme uncertainty owing to a highly dynamic, competitive market or the potential for disruptive innovation.

- The size of a business opportunity is not clear.

- High-throughput, low-changeover production can reduce your costs.

- You need to ramp up production and test markets while your permanent facilities are still on the drawing board.

- A first-mover advantage could help you gain significant market share.

If you decide that a disposable factory approach is right for you, you may need to overcome resistance from various quarters of your organization. In some companies in which the engineering culture is dominant, managers may object to this approach, citing concerns about labor relations, safety standards, and regulatory constraints. They may also consider disposable factories crude compared with big, complex ones.

One way to convince them that scale is not always the answer is to explain that a "ball-point pen" approach to organization design can liberate substantial value. It will enable your firm to capture economic opportunities that it might otherwise have missed out on or rejected. Remind them that competitors in low-cost countries have gained toeholds in global markets by going with disposable factories.

Plant engineers, in particular, will need to rethink their approach to scale and flexibility. Encourage them to shift their focus from how many permutations and combinations of products their factory can make to how the plant could be scaled *down* to serve emerging demand more agilely. The disposable factory may at first seem crude to them, but it's actually a sophisticated form of "making do."

We know that scale can deliver big competitive advantage. Now it's time to accept that you can side-step economies of scale and make great strides toward growth and profitability.

Dynamic Pricing

One issue that can profoundly affect your company's success in the future—and afford a competitive advantage—might initially seem unlikely and even mundane: pricing.

Over the last couple of years, I've observed that many companies have adopted "good hygiene" pricing practices, such as:

- Increasing list prices to match those of their competitors when their prices have been out of line

- Enforcing special charges on custom orders— charges that had been "officially" set but had not been respected by various people throughout the organization

- Establishing premium prices for "standardized specials" and quick shipments

- Up-charging for small orders that come in at quantities lower than those agreed to for the prices committed

- Changing rebate structures and follow-up mechanisms for compliance

- Repricing parts to reflect their uniqueness (up-pricing) or commodity (downpricing)

I have also seen companies address key organizational issues that relate to pricing. They've become as adept at managing pricing as they are at managing procurement or supply-chain logistics. They've put the right processes, structures, and incentives in place; clarified responsibilities; and established mechanisms for actively monitoring the effectiveness of their pricing policies.

All these activities can lead to great results, such as the addition of two to three points of earnings before interest, taxes, depreciation, and amortization (EBITDA). Clearly, building a strong pricing platform can improve a company's competitiveness. But that platform in itself won't enable them to pull even farther ahead of rivals.

The Emergency

There are several pricing strategies that go beyond "good hygiene" practices and that have significant potential for improving profitability and creating competitive advantage. Two of the best-known are *power by the hour* and *bundling*.

There are some products—such as locomotives and photocopy machines—that customers want to use but not own. These can be priced on a usage rate. To get the most from this pricing innovation, you must ensure that the usage rates actually cover your company's costs and therefore produce profits.

GE Aviation, a division of General Electric, offers an example of how the *power by the hour* pricing strategy works in its Services organization. The company's main business had been to sell aircraft engines and spare parts, but its management realized the company was missing an opportunity to generate revenues by selling maintenance. While the business will price its maintenance offerings on a per-job basis, it also offers customers long-term maintenance agreements. These agreements enable the customers to pay a set amount over time, as opposed to a large maintenance bill when their engine goes in for repair, allowing the customers to better budget their spending. These long-term agreements are also priced at a lower cost than maintenance offerings priced on a per-job basis. This requires GE Aviation to develop the best maintenance plan to reduce the repair costs and generate revenue. To do this, the company focuses on increasing the reliability of its products and also adding new technologies into its products during the repair process to ensure the engine can stay "on wing" longer.

Both GE Aviation Services and its customers benefit from power by the hour pricing. Customers say they can save as much as 10 percent on their annual maintenance costs, and GE estimates that the program typically helps airlines save from 5 to 15 percent in maintenance costs over the life of a contract.

Bundling is an effective pricing approach when a company has a broader array of products or services than its competitors do. The firm can put some of its offerings together and price the bundle so that its rivals' narrower offerings seem unacceptably expensive when customers compare the cost of all the pieces they would otherwise have to buy separately.

But bundled pricing can also be the "third rail" of antitrust activity: frustrated competitors will whine that you are unfairly exploiting your broad offering and that consumers should have the opportunity to cherry-pick suppliers—and they might sue. I won't waste space here debating the merits of this argument, except to say that it most often comes from losers.

As useful as power by the hour and bundling can be, both practices are now widely used and do not deliver the strategic advantages they once did. That's why leading-edge companies are experimenting with dynamic pricing.

Through *dynamic pricing*, a company aligns the price of its product or service with the desire of the consumer to use that product or service *at any given moment*. To do so, a supplier gathers data on its customers' use of the product in real time, then sets prices to induce certain behaviors and to cover the costs of supporting those behaviors. Dynamic pricing improves on the other two pricing innovations because it leverages extensive and very finely sliced real-time data about consumers and their behavior.

Dynamic Pricing at Progressive

Progressive Casualty Insurance is testing new approaches to pricing and marketing automotive insurance that could revolutionize the business and leave rivals gasping for oxygen. Founded in 1937, Progressive has long been an innovator in the innovation-starved insurance industry. In its early years, when most of its competitors required customers to pay an annual lump sum, Progressive allowed its insureds to pay premiums in monthly installments. Next, Progressive took on high-risk consumers that other companies preferred to ignore and, by carefully controlling its costs, was able to make those policies profitable. Third, Progressive did the repair work on damaged vehicles itself, thereby learning a lot about the relationship between costs, types of drivers, and particular kinds of mishaps.

These strategies paid off. Progressive grew at double-digit rates for thirty years, while its rivals' growth rate was in the single digits. Indeed, the company has been counted among the most profitable property and casualty (P&C) insurers for the years in which it has been a public company.

During the height of the Internet boom, Progressive became interested in a field of technology called *telematics*. Originally developed by automotive original equipment manufacturers (OEMs), telematics uses Internet and wireless technologies to enable OEMs' customers to be "wired" while they drive. It's telematics, for example, that enables drivers to surf the Web from the convenience of their vehicles. (It didn't matter to the OEMs that few jurisdictions allow drivers to watch television while they're operating a vehicle. Never mind, go online.)

Progressive saw an interesting opportunity beneath all the hype around telematics. The combination of wireless technology, global positioning systems (GPS), sensors, and the Internet could make it possible for Progressive to monitor exactly where a policyholder's vehicle was, at what time, and at what speed it was being driven. Its first-generation plan, in effect in Texas from 1998 to 2001, involved equipping cars with GPS systems and cellular technology to calculate premiums based, in part, on how much, when, and where a vehicle was driven. Policyholders who signed up for usage-based auto insurance saved an average of 25 percent on their premium.

In 2004, Progressive introduced a different usage-based program—called TripSense—in Minnesota. In exchange for a discount on their renewal policy, participants plug a data recorder into a port in their car. It collects information about the vehicle's use, including when, at what speed, and how many miles the vehicle is driven. (The device also collects information about rapid acceleration and braking, but Progressive says it doesn't use that information to calculate a discount.) The equipment does not know where a car is or has been, because it does not rely on GPS technology.

In Minnesota, about five thousand customers are using TripSense, and their average discount is about 12 percent. In January 2007, the program was expanded to Michigan and Oregon.

With such precise information, Progressive can tailor insurance rates for each policyholder. (Pricing "by the minute" is still in the research phase.)

To appreciate how revolutionary this is, consider how pricing in the automotive insurance industry currently works. For most insurers, pricing is all about averaging and de-averaging. To set your premium, insurers fit you into a customer segment for which they can knowledgeably predict the likelihood that you'll get into an accident. The company assigns you to a segment—by which it determines your premium for the year—based on your age, gender, type of vehicle you drive, where you live, how many miles you think you will drive during the year you are covered, prior reported driving violations, and so forth. Insurers measured their success by how many segments they could identify and manage. In the end, they all still "average-priced" each customer into a segment.

Progressive's use of available technologies meant that the insurer could set premiums for particular policyholders and vehicles based on their actual, real-time driving behaviors. Liability and collision costs could sink to near-zero when a policyholder's vehicle was sitting in a garage. These same costs could soar when the vehicle was recorded as speeding and swerving during rush-hour traffic near a major city.

Clearly, such individualized pricing differs radically from the average, segmented pricing that now defines the auto-insurance industry. With average pricing, it's inevitable that the segment to which the insurer assigns you will also contain some members who are at a higher risk for accidents than you are and some who are at a lower risk. In other words, some customers are more costly for the company to serve, and some are less costly. Still, all policyholders in that segment pay the same premium. This means that some people in the segment are overpaying and some are underpaying. If you're lucky, you're paying the right amount for your level of risk. (Fat chance.)

Enter telematics. Using data about drivers' behavior, an insurance company could precisely gauge a driver's risk level—at a particular moment, and over the course of an hour, day, week, month, or year. The firm could then set prices based on those risk levels. No more "Here's your premium for the year, Ms. Rodriguez."

Of course, all this would require an insurer to collect and process enormous quantities of data. But assuming the company could pull this off, the financial implications of de-averaging pricing are very attractive. According to our analysis, pricing auto insurance by the minute could result in a pre-tax jump in underwriting profitability of as much as eight points.

Equally interesting, according to one Progressive executive, policyholders using the technology have become more aware of their own driving behaviors, including their speed. Many have reported that when their speed reaches 75 miles per hour, they take their foot off the accelerator.[2] The company is committed to usage-based insurance because, as a spokeswoman explained, "It gives drivers some control over what they pay."

The Implications

If Progressive decides to aggressively market Pharmacy Benefit Management (PBM), the drivers most attracted to this offering would not likely be the company's traditional high-risk customers. Rather, they would probably be the low-risk customers of competing insurers. Why? These are the drivers who have been overpaying in their assigned segment because of average pricing. And they want a better deal.

If these customers defect to Progressive, the average risk level of policyholders remaining in the abandoned segments will go up. Thus, the cost to serve those segments would rise, which could erode the traditional companies' profits. Meanwhile, Progressive's profitability would increase as it took on lower-risk policyholders.

To combat rising costs, the best that Progressive's rivals could do would be to raise prices across the board. But that would create a whole new group of customers who were obviously being asked (without actually being asked) to pay the freight for higher-risk drivers. Mass defections might ensue. Interesting, isn't it? Imagine sticking your company's rivals with all the worst customers from your industry.

Progressive's methods could yield additional sources of competitive advantage for the company. For example, this pricing innovation is *experience intensive*—that is, the more often an organization sets prices based on actual usage and experiences a profit or loss, the more knowledge it accumulates on what drives costs and customer behavior. This is experience that other insurance companies will have to accumulate if they themselves are to be competitive. Of course, if they have visibility they can attempt to "copy" Progressive's pricing or pricing algorithms, but they will still be in follower mode. The longer it takes for Progressive's competitors to respond, the more low-risk customers they will lose to Progressive. Desperate to win back defectors, rivals might resort to lowering their prices—which would further eat into their profits. Executives at Progressive could watch as competitors got pulled into a downward spiral.

The Economics

If Progressive's technology promises to afford so many strategic advantages to companies that use it, why isn't it already widespread? For one thing, the technology is expensive. Early on, various industry participants—including auto OEMs and their suppliers—estimated that it would cost about $300 to equip a vehicle with the required systems. Today, the figure has dropped to below $100, a figure most companies still consider too high.

In the United States, state auto-insurance regulators present another obstacle. Regulators' main goal is to preserve their jobs and keep the political peace—which they do in large part by making insurance available to every driver in their state. Average pricing facilitates this wide availability by spreading the cost of insuring high-risk drivers over low-risk ones. The car monitors would expose the vastness of this deception. Not surprisingly, some of these officials have been slow to endorse this form of dynamic pricing.

In the United Kingdom, where markets are more compact owing to denser populations, things look more promising. For example, Norwich Union, under license from Progressive, is rolling out such a strategy. In 2004, the company tested the technology with young drivers, because these motorists were most concerned about high insurance rates. Participants in the pilot saved 30 percent on their premiums. Equally valuable for Norwich, the project generated enormous volumes of data: five thousand drivers recorded data on 100 million miles from more than 10 million trips. Norwich expects data-collection rates to increase by a factor of 15 within a year. Through this technology, motorists will be able to control the cost of their insurance by making choices about when they drive, what kinds of roads they travel on, how far they drive, and other factors.[3]

Who Else Is Using Dynamic Pricing?

The Progressive example is a bit rarefied, but there are other examples of dynamic pricing. Consider toll roads, which could raise tolls during busy times and lower them during less congested times to spread traffic congestion more evenly throughout the day. In January 2006, the city of Stockholm, Sweden, proposed a trial of 'round-the-clock, seven-days-a-week, dynamic pricing based on the level of traffic congestion. In September 2006, the citizens of Stockholm voted on the proposal and it won by a slim margin — 52 percent to 46 percent. Citizens who voted against adoption argued that dynamic pricing would benefit the rich and hurt the poor. Their reasoning? Those who had less control over their travel schedules— presumably lower-paid wage earners with fixed work hours—would be more likely to travel during rush hour and therefore penalized by higher tolls.

Still, the new system has already generated important benefits for the Swedish capital. Using radio frequency identification (RFID) transponders and cameras, the system has reduced traffic in the city by nearly 20 percent. In the month after the system was implemented, a hundred thousand fewer vehicles traveled on Stockholm's roads during peak business hours, and the number of daily mass-transit riders increased by forty thousand. Rush-hour traffic in Stockholm has been slashed by 22 percent—far exceeding the target decrease of 10 to 15 percent. The additional time needed to drive from one side of the city to the other during rush hour has dropped from 200 percent higher than during off-peak hours to only 45 percent higher. And pollution levels in Stockholm have decreased.

Courses of Action

As I said earlier, many companies have already done a lot to use pricing as a competitive weapon. Dynamic pricing offers the possibility of even greater competitive advantage. I encourage you to seriously consider—and soon—how you might put dynamic pricing to work in your organization:

- Make sure dynamic pricing is right for your company. A dynamic-pricing strategy should work wherever and whenever consumers are willing to wait or pay more for a product or service depending on its availability. Offerings that fit this description include hotel rooms and rental cars, restaurant seatings, and order positions for new products like passenger jets. Dynamic pricing should also work wherever information technology can remove an intermediary between consumers and a company, so that the firm receives data about its customers immediately and frequently. An example is airport parking, where the closeness to the terminal, fullness of the lot, time of day, and the length of time the vehicle is parked are important factors—and ones that a human attendant could not easily provide or process.

- Be the first mover on dynamic pricing in your industry. Then use the information you've accumulated on consumer behavior to create further advantage. For example, if Progressive used its radical pricing policy far more extensively, far earlier, and over a much longer span of time than its competitors, it would gather a lot more data on its customers. And those huge volumes of data would give it deeper and faster insight into those customers than rivals could ever hope to gain.

A Final Thought

Clearly, dynamic pricing is in its infancy, and companies interested in using it will need to carefully think through its practical implications and executional challenges. As this pricing innovation evolves and we learn more about it, I believe it will provide important advantages over innovations that are in wider use today, such as power by the hour, yield management, and bundling.

To me, one of the exciting things about dynamic pricing is that it could offer major advantages to players across a wide variety of industries. Progressive's exploration of pricing is just one example of how this pricing innovation could play out in the auto-insurance arena.

If you decide that dynamic pricing is right for your company and have the investment dollars available to experiment with it, you stand a good chance of accumulating immense volumes of detailed, valuable information about customers. And that data could give you vital advantages over your competitors. But you'll need to move fast on this—and you'll want to keep rivals off your trail as long as possible.

Embracing Complexity

There is much discussion today about the issue of complexity, particularly as it relates to the proliferation of products and services. The dominant view—as expressed in the popular media and in general conversation around the world's conference and dinner tables—is that the product and service environments have gotten so complex that most ordinary mortals have lost their ability to cope. It's time to simplify, simplify!

In business, I hear similar complaints from executives who view complexity as an enemy with which they constantly do battle. They watch as their company—usually in response to a perceived customer need and at the urging of their marketing and sales teams—adds more features and capabilities to their current products, creates variants, adds new models, enters more diverse markets, and develops additional ways to personalize and customize their offerings.

As the operational people become increasingly burdened with manufacturing, distributing, and supporting this ever-more daunting array of products—many of which are not turning much of a profit or are even losing money—they push back. Pretty soon, the internal disciplines are bickering so intensely that the noise can be heard by more than one member of the C suite. A multifunctional task force is duly formed. It spends months in investigation. The product portfolio is weeded and pruned. Costs go down and profits go up. Heroes are anointed, and then forgotten as customers are lost and sales targets are missed.

In response, marketing and sales call for more products and services, and the C suite, concerned about dipping performance results, supports them. And so the cycle repeats itself.

Yes, there is an emergency brewing that relates to complexity, but it's not about finding ways to eliminate it—it's about finding the best way to embrace complexity in order to achieve competitive advantage.

The Emergency

Complexity is a powerful phenomenon that drives many management costs, most typically overheads. My experience is that for every doubling of complexity (almost no matter how complexity is measured, just as long as it is measured and measured consistently) the overhead costs per unit being measured/ produced increase 20 to 35 percent. Companies typically try to recover their increased costs by raising prices, increasing the volume of business, or both. These recovery efforts rarely succeed, except in the very early stages of complexity escalation, when the base is low—for example, when the product portfolio increases from one to three. When a company has twelve offerings and bumps the number up to fourteen, it's tough to get back the incremental costs through price and volume increases.

It's tempting to think that complexity can be managed through simplification—by cutting, chopping, eliminating, and reducing. So many companies turn to "better forecasting"—they try harder to predict what they think customers will want and tailor their portfolios accordingly. They go in for extensive consumer research, trial and error, and very active product portfolio management—adding and pruning products and services ceaselessly and ruthlessly. However, this is a discipline that works best in fashion-driven industries—apparel, consumer electronics, high-end food, and retail. And, even in those categories, very few companies have learned to do it well.

In the past several decades, as complexity has increased—and as management science (including flexible manufacturing) has gotten more sophisticated in finding ways to manage costs and benefits—smart companies have developed many ways to create competitive advantage by *embracing* complexity. Four of them are of particular interest and are ones that your company might consider:

- Enticing the heavy spender

- Reducing complexity anxiety

- Specifying the best choice

- Searching permutations

Enticing the Heavy Spender

Heavy spenders have a natural craving for complexity. This group typically comprises 20 to 30 percent of the customers in a given category, but accounts for 70 to 80 percent of the sales. We have seen heavy spender concentrations like this in several categories, including beer, bookstores, high-end department stores, cosmetics, fast-food chains, retail stock brokerages, and kitchen wares.

Some may dismiss this observation as just another example of the old, reliable Pareto Principle, a.k.a.

the 80/20 rule. But this explanation is too simple—these consumers think and behave very differently from light spenders. They don't just spend more; they have their own expectations for product and service selection, seek a variety of types of information and service, and need a particular type of emotional engagement with the category as well.

Understanding the psychology of the heavy spender is critical to identifying the requirements for attracting them. The following factors characterize the heavy spender:

- Favorable demographics in a spending category

- Shopping as therapy

- Favorable response to "bribery," usually with frequent buying programs

- Aspiration and status seeking

- Need for affiliation

- Adventure and thrill seeking

- Changing or renewed prioritization in life

- Manic obsessions

Let's explore the psychology of a heavy spender I know, Sandra. She is a young professional, thirty-two years old, divorced, with no children, and living in

Toronto. What distinguishes Sandra from thousands of other women with these demographics is that she really, really (*really*) loves shoes. Sandra is always on the lookout for new styles, buys three to five pairs every fashion season and has more than eighty pairs in her closet. She spends over $3,000 (or 10 percent of her after-tax income) per year on her shoe collection.

Why does Sandra behave this way? She has her reasons:

"Every summer I have to purge my sandals. Summer footwear is so expressive and unique."

"I rarely, if ever, walk by my favorite stores without a peek."

"I often feel I am on mission for the right shoes for a special-occasion outfit. It is the thrill of the hunt!"

"It's an easy purchase that makes me feel glamorous."

"I have an inventory of business shoes, evening shoes, boot, winter boots, and casual shoes—in black and tan at a minimum—plus I replace my running shoes every nine months."

"The day I buy my first pair of Manolo Blahniks, I will know I have arrived."

And my favorite, "The best pick-up line that works for me is when a guy says, 'Great shoes!' He gets an automatic twenty-minute slot."

Sandra is crying out to be treated as a heavy spender: she is part of an attractive demographic, shopping therapeutic, aspires to ever-nicer shoes, and has clearly made shoes a personal and fiscal priority. When Sandra is not working, working out, or out on the scene, she spends most of her time in a three-by-two block area in Yorkville, Toronto's high-fashion area. This district is heaven to heavy spenders for shoes.

Retail formats focused on heavy spenders can be found in many consumer categories if you know what to look for. These formats are characterized by large selections, a concentration of items around lifestyle themes, lots of point-of-sale information, and very knowledgeable sales staff. They are very different from the typical mom-and-pop shops and big-box retailers. Although mom-and-pops tend to have limited selection and relatively high prices, consumers like them because the proprietors are usually quite knowledgeable and the stores are local and therefore convenient. Big-box retailers, which account for about 30 to 50 percent of a consumer category's sales, offer a wide selection of goods at very low prices but have limited customer service. The credo of most big-box retailers is to "stack 'em high, sell 'em low!" Finding a salesperson can be difficult enough; finding someone with deep knowledge in a category can be impossible. These formats don't appeal to heavy spenders except as a source for the most basic needs.

Retail formats that appeal to heavy spenders do so in several ways. They:

- Better differentiate their offerings vis-à-vis the big boxes and the mom-and-pops through wider and better product selection and by stocking brands for categories that matter most to the heavy-spending segments

- Focus their marketing efforts on categories that matter most to the heavy spenders

- Improve product selection in destination categories

- Improve signage and organization of each category to prevent walkaways—people who opt out of the process because it's too complicated or because they simply can't find what they're looking for

- Hire and train more knowledgeable sales staff for categories that appeal to their target heavy spenders

- Organize around destination categories, adding related category merchandise—a practice that also enables sales staff to become expert in all aspects of a category

- Improve the displays that showcase new products by adding experiential elements and more branding

Serving the heavy spender presents a huge opportunity to gain competitive advantage. The company that overinvests (by industry standards, anyway) in its heavy spenders and makes it expensive for them to switch to a different brand (there are many ways to accomplish this) can increase its share of this group and enjoy a revenue gain significantly greater than that of competitors that average their offerings across spender groups. The company can also increase purchase volume to the point that its costs go down relative to its competitors.

All of these measures, of course, require money. But my experience suggests that when the right heavy spenders are identified and served well, the net benefit can be huge. The heavy spender will spend more money per visit (as much as ten times more than the light spender), come in more often, and wander into adjacent categories and spend money there as well. The result is that the company can earn operating margins five to ten times higher than retailers with formats designed to serve the average sporting goods buyer. What's more, a virtuous circle can be established. Even with the higher service costs, the total costs in the heavy-spender departments actually go down because of the higher revenues. Some of the better-known names of companies that understand heavy spenders and serve them well include lululemon athletica, The Home Depot, Williams-Sonoma, Coach, Best Buy, and Shoppers Drug Mart.

There are many other categories and customer segments where smart companies are deploying, or considering, a heavy-spender strategy, including home improvement, home security, retail for seniors, road warriors, pet care, and personal care—and perhaps yours.

Reducing Complexity Anxiety

When faced with more complexity than they can deal with, many consumers will often buy a simpler and usually less expensive offering, or simply buy nothing at all. They fear they won't like the complex offering . the return process if they can't live with the product. Companies that can reduce the anxiety of dealing with complexity can gain a competitive advantage.

An interesting example is Zappos.com.

Zappos.com, founded in 1999 in Las Vegas, is an online retailer of bags, apparel, and accessories such as eyewear, jewelry, and hats—but the company is mainly known for shoes. In 2000, Zappos.com had gross sales of $1.6 million. The company projects sales of $600 million in 2007. In 2006, nearly 2 percent of consumers in North America shopped at Zappos.com.

Zappos is hardly complexity-free. It offers over nine hundred brands, one hundred thousand styles, and stocks more than 3 million items. However, the retailer does many things to reduce the customer's anxiety in dealing with the complexity of so many choices. It offers free shipping both ways—delivery and, if necessary, return. It maintains 24/7 live, free customer support. (1-800-927-7671.) And it gives a 110 percent guarantee: "If within ten days of your purchase, you notice and we can verify a lower price for the same style, width, size, and color at another retail store or online, just let us know, and we will refund you 110 percent of the difference."

Even with all these services and support systems, shoe shoppers can still feel anxiety about buying shoes they have not seen, tried on, or taken for a spin around the carpet. So, the most important aspect of Zappos.com—according to many customers I've spoken with—is the return policy. Shoppers are encouraged to order as many pairs of shoes as they'd like to try—a range of styles, or different sizes or colors in the same style. They have the freedom to consider their choices for an astonishingly long period of time. Not two weeks. Not thirty days. Not sixty days. The Zappos.com customer has 365 days to consider a purchase decision. Each shipment comes with a return courier envelope, with a return address label and prepaid shipping. All the consumer has to do is to put the shoes in the original package (in the "same condition that you received them"), slip it into the envelope, and call the courier (UPS or FedEx). On a visit to a UPS outlet in Palm Coast, Florida, I saw that, of the eight boxes waiting to be shipped out, seven were Zappos.com return cartons!

The anxiety of making the wrong choice, being unable to use the product, or of having to go through a complicated return process is reduced to zero. How many purchases have you made recently with such little anxiety involved?

Specifying the Best Choice

Shoes and handbags are not inherently complex—it's only because of the range of possibilities that consumers feel complexity anxiety. But there are many products that are, in and of themselves, complicated—

cars and computers, for example. To find the product combination that satisfies their needs and fits their budget, consumers must sift through a variety of platforms, features, variations, and options.

Historically, companies that offer such complex products have relied on salespeople to help customers determine the specifications of a product that will best suit their needs. To do so, the salespeople generally need training. They also usually receive incentives for getting their customers to close. Too often, though, these incentives are designed to encourage the salesperson to specify a product combination that is the best choice for the *company*—such as one that delivers a high profit or that helps reduce excess inventory—rather than the best choice for the *consumer*.

Customers don't like being pressured to buy what the salesperson wants to sell, but their time and patience are limited, and they rarely have the capacity to sort through all the possible combinations of features and prices themselves. If consumers are not satisfied before their patience and energy run low, they will eventually settle for the product that comes closest to what they want—or else they'll say, "Forget it."

So, companies that can genuinely specify the best choice for their customers can gain a significant advantage over companies whose customers have to do the work themselves. Early specifiers include Saturn and Dell.

In the archaic world of auto retailing, traditional dealers want the customer to buy a car that is already on the lot, and the salesperson will put a great deal of pressure on the customer to do so—offering a better price or throwing in extras to entice the customer to go with the in-stock vehicle. If the customer resists the pressure and insists on ordering a car to his or her own specifications, the sales rep will pull out a glossy sales brochure and allow the customer to select from the various options. Then a specialist at the dealership translates the selections into a series of factory codes, which are impossible for the consumer to decipher. Off goes the order, and the consumer waits. When the vehicle finally arrives, it often is not exactly what the customer expects. (My wife once ordered a car, and specified a leather interior. When the car arrived, however, the seats were cloth. The dealer offered to knock off $2,000 if we'd take it anyway. My wife said no. We waited another eight weeks to get the car we had ordered in the first place.)

Saturn introduced a no-haggle policy, and limited the available options. That allowed many dealers to create a "spec" sheet, a one-page list of all available configurations and options, prepared in such a way that the customer could actually read and understand it. Using the sheet, the buyer could simply check the desired features and the order is sent to the factory. Saturn, of course, has a limited product offering, which makes it relatively easy for the company to fit all the options on a one-page sheet. Although its narrow product range has brought some challenges to the company, the set-price, limited-options approach is an innovation that consumers like, which creates loyalty and gives the company a competitive advantage.

Dell Inc., with its online ordering system, is another early standout example of a specifier. Into the early 2000s, nonexpert consumers generally dreaded the task of ordering a personal computer. Although they understood the utility of many of the features and options, many others were almost completely mysterious: CPU speed, cache memory, sound and video cards, ports, connector types, and on and on. In a retail store, consumers could ask a salesperson for advice, but often found that the process added to the complexity of the choice, rather than reduced it. And, just as with cars, the computer salespeople wanted to push what was already in stock or whatever it was they were being "spiffed" (incented) by their boss to shovel out the door.

Enter Dell.com. The company reduced the complexity of the purchase decision process by offering a small number of starter platforms, each at a different level of price and performance. After selecting a base price/performance level, the consumer is led through a series of choices—amount of memory, size of hard drive, monitor, external storage, visual and audio upgrades, speakers, printers, keyboards, mice, and software packages. Each choice is accompanied by helpful explanations, images, and descriptions. Consumers can take as much or as little time as they like and configure and reconfigure as many times as they desire.

We conducted interviews with consumers who had purchased their personal computers at retail stores and also talked with consumers who had bought online at Dell.com. The results were strikingly different. The great majority of the retail purchasers said they were satisfied with their purchases—what else would they say, having just walked out of the store? Sometimes they admitted that they hadn't considered the purchase very carefully; they just needed something basic and cheap and grabbed whatever caught their attention. Most of them said (as they heaved a big box or two into the trunk) that they had gone for the best package they could get for the price they were willing to pay.

The Dell online consumers were also generally satisfied, but they knew much more about what they had purchased and why it was the system they really needed and wanted. When we asked about their choices of options, more often than not they said they had traded up rather than gone for the cheaper alternative. They generally bought more memory, a larger monitor, or a better printer. We estimate that, thanks to Dell's specification process, consumers spent 15 to 20 percent more on their purchases than they would have without a "specifier"—if they had simply gone for the original price/performance starter option.

More and more companies, in a variety of industries, are offering similar specifiers to consumers. You can specify your insurance policies with Progressive and GEICO and your kitchen cabinet and appliance preferences at IKEA. Even the major automakers are following Saturn's lead—today, some 70 percent of consumers use the Internet (when manufacturers have made their product data available on their sites) to research their vehicle purchase before visiting a dealer. Of course, once there, they still have to negotiate with Mr. Big and face the possibility that the car they ordered will arrive with cloth instead of leather seats. The industry still has a few outmoded practices.

Searching Permutations

Consumers, whether they are business-to-consumer or business-to-business, often find that they have a specific need that can be met by a myriad of products or services. The complexity they face is twofold: first, the very large selection to choose from and, second, the permutation of configurations within each choice. The challenge is even greater if the choices and permutations vary in price. The company that can help the consumer cope with these challenges can have a serious advantage over on its competitors.

W.W. Grainger, a distributor of industrial goods, is a great example of a company that uses very capable search engines to help its customers embrace complexity. The company has about six hundred branches throughout North America and China and serves nearly two million customers, including contractors, service and maintenance shops, manufacturers, hotels, government, health care, and educational facilities. Customers visit Grainger in search of new and replacement equipment such as compressors, motors, signs, lighting and welding equipment, and hand and power tools—as well as components and supplies. The company's print catalogue runs to more than three thousand pages, with some 130,000 products.

In 1996, Grainger began doing business on the Internet at www.grainger.com to help customers navigate its vast offering. In addition to its search engine, the site contains several expert "MatchMakers" that help would-be buyers select products that have a large number of critical attributes. My favorite is Motor Match, because I am reminded of when I was a young engineer at a major oil company. I needed to replace an electric motor in one of the company's refineries. Sitting down with several massive volumes of catalogues from the big industrial supply companies, including Grainger, I had to comb through the descriptions of all the motors to find one that best met our needs. The listings were organized by manufacturer, then by horsepower, and then by many other characteristics. When I found the right motor from one manufacturer, I would check the other manufacturers' listings to see how their offering compared, both by features and by price. The process could take hours and usually ended with a shrug and a thought, "This will do the job." Or "That's probably good enough."

Today, I can hop onto the Grainger site, access MotorMatch, and the system helps me evaluate my options by a delicious variety of criteria, such as:

- Motor type (there are seventeen types available (e.g., three-phase, capacitor start, permanent magnet)

- RPM

- Horsepower

- Kilowatts

- Volts (ranging from the obvious to the obscure)

- Enclosure (seventeen types, including open, totally enclosed, vented)

- NEMA/IEC frame (twenty-nine choices)

I hit "go" and, bam, up comes a list of all the motors available through Grainger that meet my criteria. The MatchMaker automatically narrows my options each time I enter a new specification, to make sure I never enter incompatible choices that will make me "come up dry." The other search engines on www .grainger.com enable me to search for the part I want by its application. For example, I can search for a hex head cap screw based on grade, property class, material, finish, thread size, length under head, and thread length.

The complexity remains, but now I have control over it, rather than the other way around.

A Final Thought

Many businesses whose products and services seem overly complex believe that the solution for them— and their customers—lies in simplification. Reduce the number of choices. Eliminate options. Create packages.

But embracing complexity can work for many companies in a variety of situations, particularly when:

- The customer needs and is offered a lot of choice

- The purchase decision requires trade offs

- The desired end-state can be reached along multiple paths

- Multiple end-states are possible

- The product must be "sold" rather than "bought"

- Competitors are either simplifying or ignoring the complexity phenomenon

Consumers don't inherently dislike complexity—they want to get the product or service that most closely matches their needs and budget. It's the frustration of being unable to take advantage of complex offerings that forces them to make poor (and usually lower-priced) choices or drives them away altogether.

Some say that complexity is the enemy of success in their category.

I say, love thy enemy.

Infinite Bandwidth

In recent years, I've noticed that companies are rarely short of opportunities to spend money on information technology to improve their business. And improve they have. They've outsourced call centers to countries like India and China—and achieved huge savings. They've invested in customer relationship management technology—and gained valuable new insights into who their most profitable customers are and how to keep them loyal. They've overhauled their Web sites to reflect cutting-edge design and functionality—and attracted more and better customers while gaining additional insights into their needs. And they've outsourced major business processes, such as HR-policy management, to vendors who handle those processes on a hosted Web site—gaining new efficiencies for their enterprise.

Even as companies have generated important benefits through these investments, the exciting opportunities to spend money on IT just keep coming. You're probably already being hit up for all sorts of new Web gadgets, including a CEO blog, Web 2.0, and distributed innovation (whereby companies generate ideas for new offerings with the help of suppliers and customers through blogs and interactive Web sites). And you know that these tools will soon be followed by even more remarkable ones.

The Emergency

Sure, the latest IT innovations have generated important benefits for a lot of companies. But I believe you can widen your IT "lens" to create an even stronger competitive advantage for your business. How? Think of all these alluring—if disembodied—IT opportunities as falling within one high-level conceptual framework: *infinite bandwidth*. In a world of infinite bandwidth, companies effortlessly receive any amount of information they want, in any form they need it, at any time and place, and at zero cost.

In this world, organizations that know how to leverage infinite bandwidth are more productive than their competitors, find more profitable and efficient ways of conducting business, and even create new businesses—while rivals struggle to catch up. These players ruthlessly pursue the opportunities presented by infinite bandwidth to benefit their customers and shareholders while punishing competitors.

A world of infinite bandwidth sounds incredible, doesn't it? But it's not a fantasy. That world is rapidly overtaking us as the power of data processing, storage, and analysis improves dramatically and as bandwidth and wireless technologies advance. About twenty years ago, a laptop modem could barely muster 1,200 bits per second (bps) over a telephone line. Today, low-end laptops come standard with 115,000-bps modems. Improvements in today's networks—wired and wireless alike—far exceed this change in capability as well as many others from the past decade. These emerging capabilities represent virtually infinite enhancements over previous technologies.

Yet many executives have not kept pace with this revolution. Some haven't identified ways to use technological advances to create competitive advantage and open new strategic opportunities. Others, hearing all the hype about the telecom woes and slow consumer uptake of 2.5G and 3G telephony, have discounted the importance of the latest technological feats. Still others view the new technologies as merely "cool" gadgets for managing everyday tasks, such as interrupting meetings to say goodnight to the kids over their video cell phones.

These executives ignore the promise of the bandwidth revolution at their peril. They should be carefully evaluating the many captivating technology solutions being hawked today in the context of a world of infinite bandwidth. And they should be asking themselves, "What could infinite bandwidth do for my company? Which of these new gadgets and systems will help me attain the benefits offered by infinite bandwidth? Which ones will enable me to develop strategies for outperforming competitors?"

The bandwidth revolution is analogous to the Internet revolution of just a few years ago. Then, the Internet opened up radical new opportunities in the business-to-consumer (B2C) world. Much of the excitement over the Internet was focused on the consumer, and the more arcane uses of the Internet in business-to-business went unnoticed. Only after the B2C bubble burst did the many business-to-business (B2B) opportunities presented by the Internet come to the forefront. The same is happening today with infinite bandwidth. Business leaders, distracted by the consumer and social applications that technological advances have presented, are paying scant attention to the new commercial opportunities.

There's immense value in the B2B arena waiting to be captured and used for competitive advantage. How will your company claim that value before your rivals do? In the rest of this memo, I offer some thoughts on the subject and several courses of action you might consider.

The Implications

I believe there are three increasingly potent steps companies can take to begin using infinite bandwidth to create competitive advantage:

Opportunity 1: Pursuing Operational Efficiency and Productivity

New information technologies can help you improve operational efficiency and productivity throughout your firm. Examples include broadcast e-mail, wireless taps into your company data, hosted management of your sales force, and local-area-network personal digital assistants (LAN/PDAs).

To illustrate, a major retailer recently deployed wireless LAN/PDAs throughout its network of stores. Associates used them to enter sales data and scan products on the shelves to improve inventory accuracy and timeliness of stock reordering and shelving. By placing these devices in the hands of more than fifteen thousand associates in over eight hundred stores, the retailer was able to set and track its prices based on actual on-the-shelf inventories instead of weekly sales promotion campaigns. It could also identify and immediately address imminent stock-outs. The company's reward? Significant increases in same-store and overall sales, sales per associate, and sales per square foot.

Other organizations have made similar investments—and have achieved similar results. For instance, an appliance service firm equipped its traveling technicians with devices that made it easy to determine which kind of technician would be most appropriate to handle which kind of repair or service call. This same technology enabled technicians to stock the right parts in their vans the night before a service call, to track their progress against the repair schedule, and to make adjustments in call schedules to keep customers satisfied. Thanks to this savvy use of technology, technicians' productivity improved, as measured by service calls successfully completed per day.

Of course, any increase in operational efficiency and productivity improves profitability and justifies the technology investment. But these moves don't give companies a sustainable competitive edge. Rival firms can buy similar solutions from the same venders and quickly match the front-runners' gains. The value created by any improvements through such uses of technology will melt away through price cuts and service giveaways.

Pursuing operational efficiency and productivity is obviously good, but you'll need to do more if you want to extract the most strategic value and profits from infinite bandwidth.

Opportunity 2: Creating New Business Models

As the world of infinite bandwidth comes into sharper focus, you'll have more opportunities to design new business models based on ease of information transfer. You'll be able to move data rapidly throughout your organization and exchange data with suppliers and customers, at speeds never before possible. You'll funnel information from customers and equipment directly to product managers, field service people, and design and production engineers, who together will use the data to improve their performance in real time.

For example, instead of taking months to bring a new piece of equipment up to operating specifications, your people will now accomplish it in weeks. And once the customer is using the equipment, your company will easily provide ongoing after-sales support. At first blush, this looks like merely an increase in service efficiency. But it actually represents a new business model. Through new use of technology, one of our clients in France was able to extend the role of its service force to include ongoing sales support. This freed up a portion of the company's sales force to open new accounts, while service staff tended to existing accounts.

New business models will enable you to create more sustainable strategic competitive advantage than you can gain through merely improving operational efficiency and productivity. But that's only if you can be the first mover and if you can use information technologies in innovative ways that rivals can't copy.

In Japan, the Coca-Cola Company and its bottlers own and operate one of the world's largest networks of vending machines. These machines sell a much wider variety of products than machines in North America do. In addition to carbonated products, they dispense blends of coffees as well as energy drinks in cans. As you might imagine, keeping these machines stocked is a challenge, as buying patterns vary by machine location, product type, time of day, and season.

To address the difficulty, Coke equipped these machines with technologies that enabled them to communicate their inventory status to bottlers, which could dispatch trucks immediately to restock machines with whatever fast-moving product was about to run out. Later, Coke installed technology to monitor temperature and time of day when consumers purchased certain products from vending machines in different locations. The company began varying prices based on its evaluations about what the market would bear in those specific locations and under specific environmental conditions. For instance, it charged higher prices at vending machines from which consumers bought more cold drinks on hot, sunny days.

Coke has also installed technology to enable consumers to pay for their vending-machine purchases using their mobile phones. In Japan, people employ their cell phones not only for talking but also for participating in chat rooms, playing games, searching the Web—and paying for a wide range of things, including taxis. By equipping vending machines with cell-phone payment capabilities, Coke has provided its Japanese consumers with more convenience—and has boosted vending-machine sales. And with data collected through cell-phone purchases about which customers are buying what products, the company has begun experimenting with loyalty programs.

Coke first enhanced its competitive advantage by installing vending-machine communications capabilities before rivals did and achieving new operational efficiency. But the company created a more sustainable advantage by using its network of machines in ways that competitors couldn't easily imitate. In other words, it developed a new business model when it finely tuned vending machines' mix of products and prices based on local conditions and knowledge of customers. It's not the technology Coke used that gave it a strategic advantage; it's the way the company used the technology.

Opportunity 3: Birthing New Businesses

Despite the impressive benefits to be gained by developing new technology-aided business models, you can extract even more strategic value by creating entirely new businesses that leverage the benefits of infinite bandwidth. Thanks to infinite bandwidth, companies no longer need information to physically accompany the flow of material goods. And they can reach unprecedented numbers of constituents—anywhere, at any time—with new technologies. These developments have laid the foundation for entirely new businesses.

Consider the medical-imaging industry, including radiology. Today, most of what constitutes radiology—image capture, display, interpretation, and doctor-patient consultation—occurs within the walls of hospitals and at great cost to health-care providers and patients alike. Imaging equipment is expensive to purchase, operate, and maintain. The services of the radiologists who interpret X-rays are also costly. And bottlenecks can occur if there aren't enough radiologists at a particular hospital, and at a particular time and location, to process the images that need interpretation, forcing patients and their doctors to wait to receive test results.

GE Healthcare set out to improve this situation. Its initial goal was to lower the cost of keeping its medical-imaging equipment functioning. The company attacked these costs aggressively with remote diagnostics technology. Before the use of remote diagnostics, equipment providers sent technicians out for scheduled maintenance as needed if problems arose: when a machine stopped working correctly, the hospital notified GE, and the company sent a technician to the medical center to repair the equipment.

Today, GE uses remote sensors and communication links that alert the company not only to equipment problems but also to a machine's imminent need for routine service. Based on what the sensors show about the usage patterns for a particular piece of equipment, GE can design appropriate maintenance schedules for individual machines. For example, machines in heavier use get more frequent servicing. With the preventive maintenance that the sensors enable, GE has achieved its goal of reducing the cost—for itself and its customers—of keeping the equipment running. GE Healthcare also offers tools that enable engineers to remotely monitor critical device functions, detect impending trouble, and conduct repairs before the customers even know there's a problem.

These uses of technology have helped GE improve its operational efficiency. But its competitors have begun using remote diagnostics as well, threatening to erase the advantages GE has gained. For this reason, GE has pushed further to develop new businesses that leverage infinite bandwidth and that give it a more sustainable advantage.

Interpretation of medical images offers one example. In today's world of infinite bandwidth, radiologists don't need to be located at the site where the image is created or even in the hospital where the imaging equipment, patients, and doctors are located. X-rays of a seriously ill patient in Elmira, New York, for example, can be interpreted by a radiologist at Boston's Massachusetts General Hospital, as long as she has access to technology that enables her to receive and view a digital version of the images. A physician may have several reasons for wanting a radiologist in another location to view a patient's X-rays. For instance, perhaps the radiologists at his hospital are running behind schedule, creating an unacceptable delay in interpreting the patient's X-rays. Or maybe the patient's problem requires the insights of a radiologist with specific expertise. The matching of medical images with remote radiologists can be orchestrated at a moment's notice by an advanced image-analysis center—an entirely new business. Additional new businesses could emerge from this use of technology: applications development; network investment; data collection, management, and dispersal; equipment-servicing management; and merchandising of data to researchers and medical-product and -service suppliers.

These new businesses promise not only to dramatically decrease the cost but also to improve the quality of medical imaging. First, remote diagnostics will eventually raise the average accuracy of image interpretation: as the best physicians for the problems being diagnosed are brought online, the average accuracy of all interpretations will improve. Second, as researchers mine patients' data history, the profession's overall diagnostic skills will improve. Moreover, organizations that have the strongest network of radiologists, specialists, and doctors with the highest availability and most data will gain the edge, because customers (hospitals) would be reluctant to switch to another network.

As companies like GE and Coca-Cola explore these three opportunities—pursuing operational efficiency and productivity, designing new business models, and creating new businesses—they and their customers benefit. Operational efficiency and productivity enable firms to do what they're currently doing but less expensively than before, which translates into savings for customers, too. Through new business models, organizations do what they're currently doing, but with tweaks that customers find attractive (such as paying for a vending machine purchase with one's credit card). And through new businesses, companies offer new forms of value to customers in addition to (or instead of) what they're already providing (such as medical-imaging interpretation).

The Challenges and the Opportunity

Right about now, you may be asking yourself, "If infinite bandwidth is so wonderful, why don't we hear more about it?" My colleagues and I asked ourselves the same question. To find answers, we conducted a series of interviews with equipment and service providers and their customers—usually businesses. We spoke with people at more than sixty companies in North America, Europe, and Japan, asking them what they saw as infinite bandwidth's potential value for their own businesses and their customers' businesses. The providers were from a variety of industries, including telecommunications, wireless and switching, and diversified electronics. Their customer companies also came from a broad range of industries, such as investment banking, general contracting, health care, hospitality, airport logistics, consumer goods, and pharmaceuticals. Additional customer industries included transportation, mining, travel, and utilities.

Virtually all the executives we interviewed saw infinite bandwidth as especially important in industries characterized by mobility and remoteness of people, equipment, and goods; dependence on or dispersion of enterprise intelligence; and perishability or dynamic nature of information. Many could see the potential for cost reduction and productivity improvement, as well as incremental increases in sales of existing products and services. But few articulated the potential for new business models and businesses that would come with having any amount of information they wanted, in any form they needed, at any time, in any place, at zero cost.

Moreover, many of our interviewees expressed concerns about technologies that enable infinite bandwidth. For example, an executive at a Japanese industrial firm said, "We deployed a wireless LAN in our warehouse without assessing the impact. We now have more steps than we used to." A director of theme parks noted, "We are not deploying wireless applications because we believe the technology will be leapfrogged." And a claims director at an insurance company explained, "We are now reengineering our claims process for the second time to recoup investment [in the technology]."

In summary, most of our interviewees—providers and their customers alike—were wary of adopting new, unproven technologies. They had concerns that the technologies might not be available from a single reliable supplier; might not deliver on the promise of a new business model, much less new businesses; and would become obsolete before the businesses could see a return on their investments.

Further, many of the executives we spoke with consistently underestimated the economic and strategic potential of infinite bandwidth. For some, the promise of new business models and businesses is so difficult to quantify that they can't see a way to develop a respectable business case for adopting such technologies. My sense is that people are watching and waiting to see what will happen on the infinite-bandwidth front.

What an opportunity for a forward-thinking company like yours to create competitive advantage and craft new strategies for growth!

Courses of Action

How might you best use infinite bandwidth to steam ahead of rivals—and maintain your lead? I recommend examining your portfolio of businesses and identifying those that would benefit most from new information technologies. These enterprises will likely have high-cost-to-serve business models. Such enterprises are people-intensive and rely on "feet on the street." Salespeople take information to current and potential customers, help them make the correct purchase choices, and follow up to make sure customers are happy. Examples include suppliers of electronic equipment and computer systems for corporate clients and cleaning chemicals and equipment for food manufacturers—to name just a few.

"Feet on the street" enterprises are where infinite bandwidth may help you first achieve operational efficiency and then develop innovative business models and maybe even birth new businesses. The more an enterprise in your portfolio depends on point-of-need information (especially interactivity between your company and its customers), the greater the potential for infinite bandwidth to make a difference.

To get the most from infinite bandwidth, I recommend first learning a few things about your customers. Specifically, through shopalongs and interviews, find out how they get the information they need. For example, what questions do your salespeople and customers ask each other? And how do customers research suppliers? (Do they read the business press?

Search the Internet? Ask colleagues for referrals?) Also determine how your customers use information. For instance, by what criteria do they compare several suppliers? How do they make trade-offs? How do they determine the amount of time they're willing to invest in a supplier relationship? How do they use information to make purchasing decisions? Do they buy one thing to get another—such as purchasing a skybox at a sports event not for the view and snacks but for the opportunity to safely contain a group of children?

Then, ask yourself how different parts of your organization could use infinite bandwidth technology to provide the information your customers want—in real time—and to help them use the information in the way they need. To illustrate, in an insurance company, one part of the organization provides actuarial data to set prices for customers seeking life insurance policies. The marketing department creates customer profiles, and the accounts receivable department gauges customers' creditworthiness.

I also suggest taking a hard look at attitudes toward infinite bandwidth within your firm. This brave new world is coming, and it will have enormous implications for your industry and your company. Some of the technologies required to make it happen are here; others will arrive soon. To seize the real strategic advantage (beyond mere operational efficiency) that infinite bandwidth makes possible, everyone in your organization will have to work together in new ways.

For instance, marketing and sales will need to ask logistics and manufacturing questions such as, "Customer A wants to switch from twelve units per carton delivered weekly to eight units delivered every other day. What has to change in your functions and ours for our company to meet this customer's new need? What is preventing us from making those changes? What new moves can we experiment with to improve this customer's experience with our company?"

You and your executive team will also need to summon up new levels of daring that (and I'm being frank here) are not often seen in established, successful organizations. But I urge you to get your best people thinking hard and talking at length about how infinite bandwidth could help your company pull far ahead of rivals—now and in the future. The potential for improved profitability, sustained growth, and competitive advantage that infinite bandwidth offers is too great to ignore.

Conclusion
The Longer Term

So, those are the five future strategies that you need to think hard about right now. But, it's never too early to dip into the open files and see what strategies might be worth at least some of your time and attention in the near future.

As I noted in the introduction, they fall into three categories:

1. **Faint signals.** Issues that will probably become strategies but have shown only a few, very slight signs so far. A lot of development is needed.

2. **Watch list.** Potential strategies where the sources of competitive advantage are not entirely clear.

3. **Hallucinations.** Provocative issues that are so out there they may never materialize, or at least not within this lifetime.

Faint Signals

Consider some of the following scenarios, examples of strategies that are no more than faint signals today.

Pervasive Computing

Imagine a future in which computing power is omnipresent and easily interconnected—not just a network of computers, but rather a linkage of all technology encountered in our everyday lives. This is the world of pervasive computing, where computers adapt to humans instead of humans adapting to computers.

Pervasive computing will provide an interface between humans and computing systems that will operate in the background of regular human activity. It will rely on sensors, processors, and storage devices embedded within objects used by people in their daily business and personal lives—allowing these objects to take on characteristics of computing devices.

Like infinite bandwidth, pervasive computing will be adopted in stages. First will come minor, adaptive process changes such as remote health monitors and faster payments at retail using e-wallets. Then new processes and business models will emerge, such as machines that schedule their own maintenance and storage rooms that automatically reorder stock.

Next-generation business models will then come on the scene. Think of embedded devices that can diagnose patient health and perform treatment without human intervention. Or electronic architectural drawings that can direct construction schedules.

Devices will become "smart." PDAs, cell phones, and other mobile devices will be aware of their owners' tastes and will identify products of interest to them as they shop. Smart cars will tell their drivers how to find the nearest gas station when it's needed. Computers will "understand" their users without the need for explicit, machine-language instructions.

Ultimately, computers will fade into the background of human activities.

How companies can create competitive advantage with pervasive computing has yet to be demonstrated. RFID chips are the closest thing to pervasive computing there is today, but they haven't affected any company's strategy yet even though they can potentially revolutionize supply-chain performance. Infinite bandwidth is difficult enough for executive teams to come to grips with. Pervasive computing is even more challenging.

Supply-Chain Competition

If the ultimate competitive disadvantage for a competitor that sources from Asia is the six thousand miles of ocean between it and its U.S. and European markets, the ultimate expression of a company's supply-chain prowess is that it can afford to go to consignment pricing. Companies that achieve benchmark excellence in the performance of their supply chains within their industries are able to compete in new ways. By benchmark, I mean that their order-to-delivery cycle is 2.5 to 3 times faster than that of their competitors.

With that kind of delivery speed advantage, these suppliers can ask their customers to pay for their delivered goods only after they have been used or sold through to next-level customers. This dramatically alters the economics of the supplier's customers and increases the customer's cost of switching to other suppliers who cannot deliver goods as quickly and reliably.

For suppliers operating in categories in which competition from companies offering low-cost foreign-sourced goods is a problem, the cost advantage of speedy delivery may negate their competitors' advantage of low product cost. The companies reliant on imported goods have the full carrying costs and risks of an extended supply chain that the faster competitor does not.

Virtual Competitor

In an economy of integrated value chains, competitive advantage is a game of averages.

Take costs. If a company's aggregate costs are competitive, then having a cost advantage at every step of the value chain isn't necessary: the steps are bundled together. If one step is very advantaged (such as a low-cost material or component) then it doesn't matter that the other steps are at a disadvantage because they're hidden in the averaging. But as companies deconstruct their value chains into distinct segments, layers, and markets, average advantage loses its importance. What counts is advantage in each individual piece of the value chain.

The virtual competitor de-averages competitive advantage. It seeks the most advantaged source at each step of the value chain and either owns the step or contracts with a provider at that step.

Whether de-averaging is good or bad, an opportunity or a threat, depends on your perspective. De-averaging means that companies no longer have the luxury of subsidizing poor performance in one activity by combining it with strength in others.

But de-averaging also gives companies the opportunity to stop diluting strong performance in one activity by linking it to others that perform less well. Weakness in any particular activity can become a glaring liability, but strength can become a decisive competitive asset.

Companies have always been able to outsource activities they could not perform cost-effectively themselves. Outsourcing for reasons of cost has been surging. But deconstruction goes beyond cost and beyond the support activities traditionally seen as candidates for outsourcing. Virtual competition presents an unprecedented separation of activities, including some that companies see as core pieces of their identity. It breaks down traditional industry structures, destroys old businesses, and creates new ones.

Watch List

My files contain two potential future strategies awaiting further evidence of their potential to create competitive advantage.

Competitive Networks

For a long time, networks have been a hot topic of discussion but have mostly been "of interest"—intriguing to learn about, but obstinate when it came to yielding up competitive advantage.

In the past couple of years, however, I've gathered enough evidence that I'm getting ready to move networks into the "future strategies you need right now" file. Big pharma companies like Merck are using networks to speed up innovation. Auto manufacturers like Toyota use them to respond faster to changing business conditions. Smart private equity firms, including Blackstone and KKR, are putting together merger and acquisition bids much faster than their legacy rivals, through competitive networks.

I call them competitive networks not only because they can create advantage, but because they're also very difficult for rivals to duplicate and penetrate—which makes them all the more valuable.

The case that really persuaded me is one that did not immediately seem to involve a competitive network but that, on further examination, was one of the most powerful ones I've come across. In 1997, one of Toyota's key suppliers, Aisin Seiki, suffered a terrible fire in its main plant, where it manufactured a valve used in every vehicle Toyota makes—and from which Toyota bought 99 percent of its supply of these valves. Toyota had less than a day's inventory of the valves, and the loss of supply could have caused a total plant shutdown that might have lasted for months.[4] But Toyota's incredible network sprang into action. An emergency team consisting of people from the Aisin Seiki plant, Toyota, other equipment suppliers, and component manufacturers—all of whom had operated in a network for years—quickly pulled together to attack the problem of interrupted production.

The team jury-rigged production lines in sixty-two locations and assigned inspection and distribution responsibilities. Within eighty-five hours, the first production-quality valves were delivered. About two weeks after the fire, the entire supply chain was back to full production. The plant itself was rebuilt and operating again at full capacity within five months—an unprecedented feat.

Manufacturers without the kind of competitive network that Toyota had cultivated have had far more difficulty recovering from catastrophes of similar proportions. In 1991, an explosion at the Romeo, Michigan, plant of TRW—one of the largest producers of air bags in North America—shut down production. TRW was not able to restore production at Romeo and, after a year, closed the facility permanently. The lost production and damaged customer relations were punishing.

It may seem difficult to make the leap from the problem of restoring production after a fire to the creation of unassailable competitive advantage in your company. However, think about it this way. The competitive network that Toyota relied on in this emergency is the same one that enables the company to achieve high-quality, low-cost production day-to-day. It is the same network that brings new products and product improvements on stream quickly and reliably. It is the network that has powered Toyota's steady march to becoming the number-one auto OEM worldwide in production volume and profitability (on a monthly basis Toyota has reached number one this summer). And it is the network that is creating the competitive advantage Toyota has over its rivals.

Open Source

Business concepts such as Linux are exciting in that almost-unlimited resources are applied to advancing the capability of the software. The software itself is available at no cost to those who wish to use it. One major computer system provider publicly claims that the advantage of Linux is that for every dollar it spends on Linux, others will invest $4 to further advance the software.

Almost all examples of open source are about opportunities to disrupt and even destroy existing business models. There is currently no vision of how companies will make money in the new world that lies beyond the disruption. Instead, we are all expected to want to "take the streets" from the occupying troops of legacy corporations. Power to the people!

For open source to be a sustainable business concept, someone will have to demonstrate how competitive advantage can be created and sustained. Red Hat may be doing this. Red Hat's model is to be a central player in the Linux feeding frenzy, but to distinguish itself from others with its ability to provide service after Linux sales. At this point, however, the competitive advantage of Red Hat comes from this rather conventional source—service—rather than the promise of open source itself.

So we must wait and see.

Hallucinations

Hallucinations result from playing mental games about possible sources of competitive advantage for which there are currently no corporate examples. You are not likely to find such hallucinations in *Harvard Business Review* because there are no case studies to cite. But hallucinations are worth pondering.

Zero Cost of Capital

More and more senior executives are complaining about the challenge of competing with companies that behave as if their capital were free and unlimited. Today, these competitors are often Chinese, but we have heard complaints about companies from other countries, including the United Arab Emirates.

This complaint is not new. It was levied against competitors from Korea in the 1990s and from Japan in the 1980s.

Responses to this complaint include, "There is no such thing as a zero cost of capital." "You're calculating your competitors' cost of capital wrong." "It's unfair." And, "This just means you have to be an even more effective competitor." None of these responses is very actionable.

The real issue may not be the cost of capital at all. Instead, zero cost of capital is perhaps another way of saying that the competitor's investment return horizon is much longer than your own. If two competitors have the same cost of capital but one has a return horizon of a year and the other ten years, the ten-year competitor will seem to be behaving as if its cost of capital were zero.

Are there solid reasons why one company's investment return horizon should be shorter than that of a competitor? If there are, then the only option it has is to cash out: sell market share or sell the business to the competitor with the longer investment horizon.

If there are no solid reasons for a shorter investment horizon, then ways to match the investment horizon and cost of capital of competitors must be found. There are proven ways to lower a company's cost of capital, among them increasing debt and reducing dividends to fund growth, de-averaging the capital structure to match division structures by competitor, financing the company on certain stock exchanges, ensuring that capital productivity is very much higher than that of competitors by enhancing

111

asset productivity, deconstructing the business to outsource the capital-intensive portions, and dramatically improved expense productivity such as innovation to cash.

Matching investment return time horizons is tougher. Doing so probably means going private but probably not with a private equity firm (a.k.a. leveraged buyout firms). Whatever these firms like to say, their money is not patient.

Is it possible to change the mix of investors in a company from those whose money is "hot" to those whose money is patient? This would likely require delivering the kind of asset and profitability growth that attracts patient money. There are vast pools of patient money. Pension funds are in there duking it out with hedge funds for today's earnings. They are also looking for returns that will be delivered in future years to match the timing of their future pension obligations. They do this today with bonds, real estate, and infrastructure investments. Would they do so for the right corporate strategy?

Managing Uncertainty

Can a company create competitive advantage by managing uncertainty better than its competitors? In the chaotic world most companies exist in, is there an opportunity to create competitive advantage by anticipating uncertainty better and responding faster than competitors? The answer has to be "yes." Remember the saying, "In the country of the blind the one-eyed man is king"?

So, is an aspiration of being better at anticipating uncertainty and being more agile at responding to uncertainty realistic? I think so. Companies are already doing so but people do not see their behavior in this light. Southwest Airlines dramatically reduces the impact of operations uncertainty on its business with the standardization of its fleet on the Boeing 737, its goal of a twenty-minute gate turnaround, flexible work rules, and point-to-point scheduling model. For example, in the hub-to-hub model preferred by most legacy carriers, one late plane in yields four late planes out!

In the next few years, successful companies will distinguish themselves by managing uncertainty better than do their competitors. The very best will *create* uncertainty for their competitors to struggle with— and there will be hell to pay by those who fall behind.

A Final Thought: Finding Faint Signals Yourself

I'm tempted to take you through the elaborate process we use to identify ways to disrupt your industry and your business. To be good at consulting, we need these frameworks to assure clients that working with us is "safe." Kind of like the checklists the pilots use to avoid oversights, anticipate problems, and protect your (and their) lives.

But I am not going to do that (at least not in this memo). Instead I'm going to borrow an observation made by a friend, former BCG colleague, and CIO at General Electric, Gary Reiner. After being at GE for more than a decade, Gary told me that he no longer had any use for consultants—that all the new things GE could learn could be found at other companies. In particular, Gary said, GE's people are always looking for companies that are growing faster and are more profitable than their competitors. When they find one, they hop into their fleet of corporate jets and choppers and go off to look for insights, do benchmarking, and share best practices.

My colleague Tom Hout and I have done some research that suggests that Gary is actually on the right track (not that he needs another boost to his self-confidence). Tom and I started with a Harvard Business School analysis of new management ideas and practices introduced in the past seventy-five years.[5] We updated it with data gathered from various sources, including *Fortune* and *BusinessWeek* surveys, as well as our own observations. Not very scientific, maybe, but I guess that's one reason Tom and I are not academics. We grouped the innovations into seven categories: Leadership & Organization, Managing People, Sales & Marketing, Technology, Processes & Competition, Measuring & Capturing, and Corporate Development & Finance. In all, we counted forty innovations in the last twenty-five years alone.

Of those forty innovations, we gave consultants credit for being the first to identify seven of them; academics came up with nine; and industry got credit for twenty-four! (I have to add that many of the industry innovations were helped along by astute observation and analysis from consultants and academics.) So the lesson is that the faint signals I speak of are likely to be found in the world around you.

When we reflect on the executives who seem best at staying ahead of their competitors, we see patterns. They start with "tools," but move quickly to unique framings and actions. The process is "animal": part instinct, part intellectual, part social. An effective strategy-development process favors:

- Easily accessible learning sources

- Messages that bear directly on the situation

- Advisers who appear capable of directly helping now

- Experience at the "rock face" with companies that are trying new and different things

The best executives look far beyond their own industries and competitors for insight. They seek winners in other industries who may have found a new way of operating and competing that can be transplanted into their industry to the great confusion of others and then they "plagiarize" the idea. Or they come across an anomaly, understand its implications and use the insight to drive the business to new levels of performance. (You can read more about this in my earlier book, *Hardball*.[6])

Along the way, they are sure to catch the faint signals of a new world in the making. Then the hard part comes: do they wait and see, or do they see and make the others wait?

Notes

1. Chris Zook, "Finding Your Next Core Business," *Harvard Business Review*, April 2007, 75.

2. Kevin Maney, "Big Insurer Progressive Launched Its Trial, Dubbed TripSense, in Minnesota Last August," *USA Today*, August 3, 2005.

3. Lara Williams, "Insurer Opens Up Pay-per-Drive," *Computing*, October 12, 2006.

4. *Harvard Business Review* provides a great example of this benefit (Philip Evans and Bob Wolf, "Collaboration Rules," *Harvard Business Review*, July 2005, 96–105).

5. Supplement to *Harvard Business Review*, September–October 1997.

6. George Stalk and Rob Lachenauer, *Hardball: Are You Playing to Play or Playing to Win?* (Boston: Harvard Business School Press, 2004).

About the Authors

George Stalk is a Senior Partner and Managing Director of The Boston Consulting Group. He has consulted to a variety of leading manufacturing and service companies throughout the world. For over a decade, George worked and lived in Japan, where he first revealed the sources of Japanese competitive advantage in cost, quality, and—most important—time, leading to BCG's breakthrough thinking on the use of time as a competitive weapon.

From 1998 to 2003, George led BCG's worldwide innovation efforts—funding and managing thrusts into almost all aspects of e-commerce strategy, pricing innovation, and identifying and exploiting strategic discontinuities. His work yielded insights into managing channel conflict, complexity, using broadband wireless to create competitive advantage, organizing for e-commerce, "power by the hour," and pricing. Today, he works to integrate emerging Chinese threats and opportunities into the competitive strategies of clients.

George coauthored *Competing Against Time, Kaisha: The Japanese Corporation, Breaking Compromises, BCG Perspectives on Strategy,* and *Hardball.*

George lives with his wife and six kids on a farm outside of Toronto.

John Butman is an author and collaborating writer whose credits include the *New York Times* bestseller *Real Boys: Rescuing Our Sons from the Myths of Boyhood*; the *Boston Globe* bestseller *Townie*, a novel; and the *BusinessWeek* bestseller *Trading Up: The New American Luxury.*